Who's Huckleberry Finn?

Wendy Greene

Copyright © 2021 Wendy Greene
Published in 2021 by Wendy Greene

The right of Wendy Greene to be identified as the Author of this Work has been asserted by her in accordance with the Copyright, Designs and Patents Act 1988.

All rights reserved. No part of this publication may be reproduced, stored in a retrieval system or transmitted, in any form or by any means, without the prior written permission of the publisher.

ISBN: 978-1-80049-637-8

Design and Print management by Verité Design.
www.veritecm.com
Tel: 07796 172659

Front cover illustration © Bob Bond 2021

Printed in England

Jules . . .

Jules fired up his laptop. Mum and Auntie Mo had made it pretty clear they wanted him out of the way. They'd given each other knowing looks before sending him up to tidy his room. They'd even given him some squash and three chocolate biscuits . . . three!

The screen came to life. Jules typed in his password, brought up the net and went straight to Matesbook. Without hesitation, he clicked 'Full List'.

A box on the screen gave the message 'Jules, you have no Mates online.' All his online mates were too busy to chat. They couldn't know he was online, but he took it as a personal snub.

He gazed out of the window. The street was quiet for a Saturday. The postman pushed his trolley past the house without stopping. Across the street the Goldsmith twins were having a water fight with the sponges their Dad had been using to wash his treasured Jaguar.

A soapy sponge missed its target and landed 'splosh' on the newly polished bonnet. The boys froze. There was a shout from inside the garage and they scuttled round to their back garden.

Jules looked back at the screen. 'Eugene is online and ready to chat'. No. Not Eugene. Geeky Eugene from school. Jules had only put him on his Mates list after the Headmaster had that chat with his class about cyber bullying and how unfair it was to exclude some people from your Matesbook or Mygang group. After all, he had tactfully pointed out, it wasn't as if you were inviting them round to your house.

Jules knew Eugene's Mum had been up to the school that morning. He knew Eugene had no friends. Eugene was a bit weird but harmless, so Jules didn't think it would hurt to include him.

Reluctantly he responded and chatted aimlessly for a couple of minutes before declaring he had to go and do something for his Mum, and signing off.

Tidying his bedroom suddenly seemed like the most interesting option available. And it would stop Mum nagging.

Half an hour, three biscuits and two tidy cupboards later, Jules began to wonder what on earth Mum and Auntie Mo could be talking about.

He drained the last of his squash and carried the glass and plate down to the kitchen. The lounge door was opening. He dived into the downstairs cloakroom.

'Come into the kitchen and talk to me while I make another pot of coffee,' Mum was saying.

Auntie Mo's high heels clattered across the wooden hallway to the kitchen.

'Well at least there's a coach I can get to visit after the move. If you'll have me Claire.'

'Oo, let me think . . . ' chuckled his mother.

Without thinking Jules flushed the loo which drowned out the conversation. He opened the door and started back upstairs.

'All right love?' called Claire.

'Yes. I just came down to er . . . get my homework,' he replied, and immediately regretted it. Now he would have to spend half an hour actually doing it.

'Good boy.'

Mum was delighted. She usually had to nag all weekend.

Once out of sight, Jules stopped to listen again. So his Aunt was moving house. Maybe she'd met a new man. But what followed confused him.

'So why such a remote village when you're such a townie?'

That was Auntie Mo's voice.

'It was Dilys who put me on to it,' replied Mum.

Dilys . . . that's Eugene's Mum!

'It'll be a big change for Julian but I know he'll love it once we . . . '

The lounge door closed. The two women were still talking but the words were muffled. They'd mentioned Julian . . . did they mean him or his Dad? Could it be his family moving and not Auntie Mo?

Jules, back in his room, took out the maths sheet that was his homework. He read it through twice but the words weren't going into his brain, which was far too busy thinking about Mum's words.

The computer screen had gone to sleep. He hit the enter key violently. Eugene was still online, and asking to chat with someone.

An idea struck Jules. He could ask the old brainbox about the homework. He wouldn't ask for the answers, just get him to explain the questions.

Eugene was delighted to be asked. His explanation almost made Jules wish he hadn't asked. It suddenly seemed so simple.

'I be glad when break up 4 summer,' typed Jules.

'Me 2,' replied Eugene, 'we moving.'

Jules was stunned. None of this made sense.

'Meet in corner shop 10min,' he typed. And without waiting for a reply he switched off his laptop and ran downstairs.

'Can I go and get my Saturday sweets please?' he called to Mum from the hallway.

'OK, but don't be long – and don't eat them – we're having lunch soon.'

Jules went out the back door, past the shed and out to the pavement. Since his tenth birthday, Mum and Dad had allowed him to go to the corner shop for his sweets. At first it had felt a bit scary without a grown-up, but the shop staff knew him so he soon felt confident. He even worked out how much change he should get, which usually wasn't much. He always put the spare coins in a pot in his room to save for something special.

Eugene was in the shop already and was choosing a comic. Being diabetic, he wasn't allowed to buy sweets, as they made him ill.

'I can't be long.' said Eugene, 'We're having an early lunch and then going to see our new house.'

Jules felt his tummy go a bit wobbly.

'Where is it? It can't be far if you're only going for the afternoon.'

'No, we're staying in a B & B tonight. The new house is in the country but I don't know where it is. The village is called Dean's Creek.'

'Eugene . . . I think we're moving there too. I heard Mum say something and she said your Mum gave her the idea.'

Eugene's face lit up. Behind his thick glasses his blue eyes actually sparkled and a smile spread over his lips.

'Wow. That's magic Jules.'

'I don't know for certain, but it's just that I heard . . . '

'It all makes sense now. When Mum told me I kicked off because I wouldn't know anyone, but then she said that might not be true and that anyway I'd make new friends – even though she knows that's not easy for me.'

'Well maybe it would be good to have new friends,' said Jules, suddenly worrying he'd be stuck with the one classmate he'd never choose as best mate.

Eugene was painfully aware he wasn't popular at school but nodded, adding, 'Maybe they'll be more appreciative of my talents.'

Eugene had made a joke. Jules looked at him for a moment and smiled. Maybe there was another side to Eugene after all.

At least being good at homework was one way to get people to talk to you. Jules thought it must be the same for rich and famous people. They had lots of other people around them all the time, just because they were rich or famous. But they weren't mates, were they?

'You've gone quiet,' observed Eugene as he paid for his comic.

Jules counted out his sweet money.

'Sorry. It's all a bit of a shock.'

Eugene was already at the door.

'Gotta go, Jules. See you at school.'

Back at home, Jules found Mum in the kitchen heating a pan of soup while Auntie Mo sliced up French bread and cheese.

'Wash your hands love.' called Mum, 'Lunch is ready.'

Still in a bit of a daze, Jules obliged. He decided to ask Mum outright.

'Mum, I've just seen . . . '

'Get the butter would you?'

'When I was at the shop . . . '

Clatter, clatter went the cutlery on the kitchen table. Jules sighed. Maybe this wasn't the moment.

The soup was delicious and the French bread lovely and crunchy.

'So Jules,' began Auntie Mo, 'who did you see at the shop?'

Jules looked up from his bowl. His Auntie always noticed him and always showed an interest in what he did. He sometimes felt Mum and Dad didn't notice him at all. Not as a person who might have something interesting to say.

He flashed a smile at her.

'Eugene from school,' he replied.

The two women exchanged glances.

'He's moving. They're going to see the new house today and it must be miles away 'cos they're staying over.'

'Only about 50 miles,' said Auntie Mo, and she flinched as her big sister kicked her under the table.

'Sorry, Claire,' she continued, 'I forgot.'

Jules looked from one to the other.

'What's going on Mum?'

'I was going to wait 'til your Dad got home but I suppose it won't hurt to say. We might be going there too.'

'To stay?' asked Jules.

'To live. It's not definite. I've been talking it over with Auntie Mo because she might buy our house and live here with your Gran.'

'Oh,' was all Jules could say.

Auntie Mo laid a hand on his wrist.

'It will be a great adventure for you. And if your friend Eugene's going to be there . . . '

Jules dropped his spoon into the empty bowl, blinked back tears and ran upstairs.

'What did I say?' Mo asked Claire.

'Eugene's the class swot. Very bright but not popular. Do you remember Donny Preston in your class at school?'

Mo nodded. 'I'll go up and see if he's OK.'

Auntie Mo knocked on the door. Jules grunted and she walked in to find him face down on his bed.

'Sorry, mate.' she began. 'I didn't mean to upset you. If you do move you'll soon make friends. And don't be too hard on Eugene. He can't help being brainy and I expect he's a bit lonely. Your Mum and I once knew a boy called Donny. Brilliant at science and maths but useless with people. But now he earns a fortune and is married to a doctor. He's really happy and has lots of friends.'

Jules knew this was meant to cheer him up and he was grateful. He sat up and hugged his Aunt. He'd miss her weekly visits. She was a lot younger than his parents and much more fun.

'Can I come back and stay with you in the holidays?'

'Well of course, but I think it would be fun if I came to Dean's Creek and you could show me around.'

Jules nodded. There was nothing in Densbridge he could show her that she and his parents hadn't explored as kids. In fact they were always moaning about their favourite haunts being built on or turned into car parks.

'Come on,' said Auntie Mo, 'let's go downstairs and Mum can show you the brochure.'

Down in the sitting room, Mum was laying out tea cups and more chocolate biscuits. This was more bribery, of course, but he wasn't going to complain.

On the sofa was a glossy brochure for Dean's Creek Development. The cover showed a close of modern houses, with neat lawns and flowerbeds.

Your new life in the country starts here, it claimed.

Inside were pictures of rooms and a view across a little river. It did look interesting. Jules looked back at the cover. There was an arrow in biro above one of the houses. It was linked to the next one but only by an upstairs bedroom, below which was an archway leading to garages.

'That's ours,' Mum confirmed.

* * *

It was the middle of June. A week since Eugene had come into school brimming with excitement, looking for someone, anyone who would listen to him. He found Jules and was surprised not to receive some excuse as to why he had to dash off and do something more important.

Jules listened, his tummy doing that fluttery thing again. When Eugene let him get a word in edgeways, Jules told him his parents had decided they would also be moving to Dean's Creek.

'We're going to see the house next weekend,' he said, 'and we'll move in the holidays so we'll both start the new school in September. I think your Mum told mine that we're moving a week after you.'

'Wow, that's quick! It took us six months to sell our house.'

'Auntie Mo's buying ours and she didn't have to sell anything, so it was easy peasy.'

'Quiet now,' called Mrs Henshaw, 'I want to call the register. Then I think Eugene Miller and Julian Petts have something to tell us.'

The boys looked at each other. Neither was sure he was ready to make an announcement. It was all a bit new, and Jules hadn't seen the place yet. Even worse, he knew his classmates would make jokes about Eugene being his new best mate.

As the week progressed Jules began to feel excited about the visit, especially after hearing Eugene's description of the new estate and surrounding countryside. He was even allowed to choose the wall colour for his new bedroom. Yes it would be an adventure.

* * *

August arrived and Eugene and his family packed up and left. Jules was in limbo. Most of his belongings were packed up in boxes. His mother had taken three bags full of toys and clothes he had grown out of to the charity shop. There were no longer pictures and photos on his walls and he suddenly felt very lonely. Who'd have thought he'd miss Eugene. His other mates had stopped calling and he'd given up trying to chat online. He'd ignored the nasty comments at school on the last day. There was more to Eugene than he'd originally thought, and he would, for a while, be his only friend in Dean's Creek. The two boys still chatted on line and Jules looked up Dean's Creek on Google Maps. The new estate wasn't on there, just a building site but he did find the school.

The final week seemed to drag by, although his parents kept saying they didn't have enough time. They had dismantled and packed the computer. He offered to help, but they just told him to keep out of the way. Finally the removal lorries arrived, quickly transferring the contents of the house in to two vans, and set off for Dean's Creek. Into the boot of the car were packed the vacuum cleaner, kettle and a box of essentials – like tea and biscuits for the removal men. Jules sat in the back surrounded by last minute packing and when they set off he turned and waved goodbye to Auntie Mo and Gran.

The journey was not too bad, and they stopped for a snack in a lay-by. As Mum and Dad chatted about the house and how to organise the boxes they'd spent weeks filling and labelling, Jules sat quietly in the back. He was going to miss his old mates, though once they knew he was going – and going with Eugene – they'd seemed to ignore him. In fact, he began to realise how awful they'd all been to Eugene. He did use big words, and he always won the spelling tests, but that just meant everyone else was jealous, didn't it? Dad had suggested that it was wrong to talk about 'winning a spelling test', but Jules reckoned no-one would bother learning them if there was no prize at the end of term. Mrs Henshaw was well aware that Eugene was way above the rest of the class, so gave three prizes – first, second and most improved.

As they drove up to the new house, Jules saw Eugene waving from the bedroom window next to his. He seemed so happy and didn't look as pale as usual. Julian opened their new front door and Claire started directing the removal men to the various rooms. Eugene and his mother appeared at the door.

'Hello,' called Dilys, 'Is there anything you need? Cup of coffee? Extra hand?'

'Come in,' Claire called from the kitchen, 'I've just put the kettle on myself. Those men are gasping – and so am I! Would you like one?'

Jules grabbed a couple of sugar-free juice cartons from the box on the kitchen table and took Eugene up to show him his room. The bed had just been placed by the window and Julian threw the bedding on to it.

'Job for you lads, then you can come down and have a chocolate biscuit. And Eugene we remembered and bought something you can have too.'

Eugene beamed. At last, someone outside the family who understood his diabetes. They quickly spread out the sheet and duvet, which had been rolled up at the old house with the pillow tucked inside. Jules threw the pillow in the vague direction of the headboard and they bolted downstairs to where the grown ups were. Claire was handing out cups to everyone.

'Mum,' said Eugene, having scoffed down his special biscuits, 'can I have the key and take Jules to see my room?'

Dilys handed over the key with a warning not to make a mess and the boys were off like a shot. Eugene's house was a mirror image of Jules's. The two boys' bedrooms joined, over the archway to the garages.

'This is my lookout post,' enthused Eugene, 'I can watch everyone in the Close and they all come over and speak to me. I can tell you all their names if you like. It'll be great. We can stick our heads out of our windows and chat.'

Having exhausted Eugene's things to look at, they returned next door to find the first van empty and all the men going off to find somewhere to eat. With all the kitchen goods stowed away, Claire thought she ought to make some sandwiches but Dilys said she'd made a large beef stew, and invited them all in to share it.

'There's plenty for everyone and I'll put some in the fridge for Tom so he can have some when he gets back. He wants to join a local cricket team and has gone over to meet them all at a nearby match.'

Julian made a mental note to speak to Tom about cricket as soon as possible. It was a game he loved to watch, and maybe, at local level, he could pick up where he'd left off when he was a single man.

Lunch over and the rest of the furniture and boxes stowed indoors, the Petts family waved goodbye to the removal men, closed the front door and flopped into their favourite chairs. The next day was Sunday and there would be plenty of time to unpack clothes, books, ornaments and so on. Now all they wanted to do was watch TV – which, after a quick retune, picked up the local signal strong and clear – and later to eat sandwiches and drink tea.

For the first time ever, Jules opted for an early night.

Exploring

After all the anticipation and excitement of the move, Jules slept like a log but woke at 7am, taking a few moments to realise where he was. His room had two windows, one at the front which was wide and looked down the length of the Close. The one on the other side of the room was smaller, with just one long window and a fanlight, overlooking the driveway and garden. Jules hadn't had time to pay it much attention yesterday and Mum had put up the curtain which she'd pulled across before he went to bed. He drew back the curtain and looked out. To his right was a wall which was the outside of his bedroom alcove and the bathroom with its frosted glass window. To the left he could see the same arrangement in reverse on Eugene's house. His room and Eugene's sat above the archway leading to the garage compound. On either side of the driveway he could see overgrown gardens. The houses had been built on unused land, so what he saw was the remains of the field that was now Dean's Close. He heard two knocks on the wall and realised Eugene was trying to get his attention. He knocked in reply then ran to the front window and looked to his right. Eugene's window opened.

'Put your phone on,' called Eugene and Jules rummaged in his bag, pulled out the phone and soon picked up a message from Eugene, saying 'meet after breakfast to explore'. He sent a smiley face back.

Claire had cooked bacon and tomato, and the toast popped up as Jules arrived at the table.

'You're up, great.' said Claire, surprised to see him washed and dressed without being told. 'I didn't want to wake you. I've made a cooked breakfast, as lunch might be a bit late. Your Dad and I have to go to the next town to do a big food shop. I don't suppose you want to join us?'

'No, Eugene texted and we're going exploring.'

'Well be careful and don't stray too far. Be back for lunch at 2, or earlier if Eugene has an earlier lunch. I've given Dilys a spare key for emergencies, but you can borrow it to let yourself in if we're not back. Just be sensible.'

'I will,' Jules assured her.

Eugene was already in his front garden when Jules left the house. He indicated the archway beneath their bedrooms and they walked through to the garage compound.

'Along here,' Eugene pointed, 'there's a passageway. I've only been down it a little way on my own. It seems to lead to a riverbank.'

The boys ran along the passageway which led past the backs of other houses, giving access for dustmen. Eugene pointed out one house with an immaculate garden.

'That's Mr and Mrs Bishop's house. They were the first to move into the Close, so they've been doing the garden for the past two months. They're OK – quite old, but they both still go out to work all day.'

Ahead of them was a line of trees. Jules could see a distinct path off to their left which Eugene said was a shortcut to the shops. There was a cluster of buildings in the distance, probably once barns.

Ahead was a stile, which the boys climbed over, and a muddy path through a small copse. On the other side, where trees turned to large shrubs, the path joined another running by a river. To their right they could see a bridge leading to the other bank beyond which was a field of wheat.

As they strolled along the path, they chatted about their hopes and concerns of living in a new town – though as yet it was just a new development with a shop and post office at the far end, which Dilys had told them was a general store, run and owned by a Mrs May. The store served the small village of Granfold which would become part of the new town once completed and the full range of amenities up and running. They would even have a Mayor, though the planners had to guarantee not to destroy the village feel.

The warm sun on the exposed riverside path had dried up the mud. The path was several feet above the water and was edged by vegetation that made it difficult to see down to the water. After a short distance they noticed a gap where someone had hacked out steps down to a small grassy area.

They climbed down carefully using the branches to steady themselves.

'This is great!' shouted Jules, 'Look there are fish in the river. Maybe we could catch one. I've got an old rod in the garage – at least it was at the old house, so I suppose it's in the new one.'

'It's so peaceful,' commented Eugene perching on an old tree stump, 'and there's a place over there that would make a great camp.'

The boys set to work weaving the softer branches together to make a little room in the shrubs at the bottom of the steps. If anyone walked along the opposite bank, you could hide and not be seen, but if anyone ventured down the steps, they could see in quite easily.

'We need some kind of door,' said Jules and they went through several not very practical options before deciding to stop thinking and eat their mid-morning snacks. Eugene pulled out an empty brown paper bag for their rubbish and put it back in his rucksack. His parents had brought him up to be very eco-minded and one of the attractions of the new house was the solar panelling on the back.

After a while Jules hit on a plan. Towards the bottom of the steps and just above the camp was a young weeping willow. Its branches were supple enough to bend and the leaves hung down like a curtain.

'Tomorrow,' he suggested, 'we'll get some strong string and see if we can make a door but without cutting the branches. I think between us we could pull some over the entrance and tie them to the other side. Then we could use the string to pull it down if someone came along.'

'Brilliant, but for now let's explore this bank and see how far along it goes.'

The grassy bank became narrower but still wide enough to walk along. Above them they could just see the path between the stems. It was quite steep but, at a pinch, possible to scramble up on hands and knees. With the earth being still damp, they decided the steps were a better bet. The path came to an end soon after and they turned back.

'Watch out, someone's coming,' whispered Jules, and Eugene grabbed him and pulled him down out of sight. Some people were walking along the path above them.

'This is just awesome,' said one of them, a boy of about thirteen, 'I wish we didn't have to go back to New York.'

'Don't even talk about it bro,' commanded a younger girl.

'Americans,' whispered Eugene as he peered after them. 'There's another boy, about our age. He's not talking so I don't know if he's from around here. I think they may be staying with him. I think I've seen him at the shops.'

'Should we call out to them?'

'Best not. We want to do our own exploring, don't we?'

'I suppose so,' replied Jules, though he would have liked to talk to them about New York. But he understood what Eugene meant. They didn't want the guided tour before they'd had a chance to explore. Then the Americans turned and retraced their steps, so the boys squeezed themselves into the undergrowth until it was safe to leave.

'Kingfisher,' whispered Eugene, and they both watched the brightly coloured bird as it dived into the river and emerged with a fish.

'Now that's awesome!' said Jules in a mock American accent.

Eugene realised it was almost one o'clock.

'I have to go home for lunch. I must have regular meals to keep my sugar levels steady. Maybe we could come back later.'

As they walked back along the high path, Jules pointed out the place they might be able to climb up. It was the only point from which you could catch a clear view of the river before reaching the steps.

As they retraced their steps to the Close, Jules turned to Eugene and said, 'We were rotten to you at school, weren't we?'

'You were OK. Some of them just went along with the bullies. Bullies are cowards who have to hurt other people to look big. That's what my Mum says.'

Jules agreed and said he wouldn't let it happen at the new school. They paused before going into their houses and looked at each of their new gardens in turn, agreeing to offer to help turn both into something spectacular.

Once home the boys discovered that their parents had planned a joint picnic tea at a local beauty spot, and although thoroughly enjoyable, it was not an adventure. That would have to wait another day.

Gone fishing

'Right,' said Julian at breakfast, 'I'm off to start my new job. Wish me luck. Jules come out to the garage with me, would you? Then you can lock the door after I've driven out.'

As the car drove under the arch, Jules waved to his Dad then turned back to the garage. Instead of locking the door, he went inside and soon found his old fishing rod. It looked very small now, but beside it were two larger ones and a box of flies. Eugene appeared and called to him.

'In here,' Jules shouted. 'Can you wait here a minute while I go and ask Mum if we can borrow the rods?'

Eugene agreed, but Claire was not prepared to loan out her husband's rods without his permission, even though it was years since he last used them. However, it was agreed that Jules could text his father to ask, though he wouldn't answer until he arrived at work. The next fifteen minutes felt like hours, but eventually Julian rang his son and gave permission but with a warning not to break them.

'I'm glad you and Eugene are having fun. Sounds all very Huckleberry Finn to me.'

Jules turned to Eugene.

'Who's Huckleberry Finn when he's at home?'

Eugene shrugged and helped Jules extricate the rods from the rack at the back of the garage. They locked up and went back to collect their rucksacks before heading off to the river.

As they walked through the copse, they met an old lady with a small dog.

'Going fishing lads?' she asked, 'My old man used to fish this river, right up 'til he died last year. Eighty he was, but determined to catch one particular fish. He'd watched it grow and it seems it's still around. Huge great thing. He had a special little place he went to. Even made steps down to it when he got too old to slide down the bank. Good luck!'

As she walked on the boys looked at one another. So that's how the steps got there. Fishing had suddenly become an even bigger adventure. Maybe they would catch the illusive fish. But on arriving at their camp they soon realised the river was running too fast for them to even see a fish.

'Did you find any string,' asked Jules.

'Yes, Dad let me have some of his garden twine. It's pretty strong. He used to train trees along the wall at our old place, but here it's all different, so he just wants one cherry tree in the middle.'

They put their bags inside the camp and looked at the willow tree. Very soon they found a couple of suitable branches, tied them together with the string and gently pulled them down until the curtain of leaves covered the entrance. Eugene took some scissors from his bag and cut the string long enough to hang down when the door was up. Then they found a suitable trunk on an overgrown shrub and tied the string firmly around it.

Eugene checked the time on his phone and declared it to be snack time, so they settled down with their food and drink. They were just packing away the rubbish when they heard shouting from the other bank. Carefully they parted the leaves and peered out. Across the river they saw three boys, who seemed to be shouting some sort of gang chant.

'Moorheads forever. We rule the river.'

After a few times, a man walking towards them ordered them to behave. Amazingly they stopped chanting and continued in silence. The biggest boy was probably about thirteen but looked tough in his rugby shirt and jeans. Beside him walked a smaller boy, about eight. Every gang leader has a small sidekick to make them look bigger and to do their bidding.

The third boy walked behind. He was wearing a cap and denim jacket over black trousers that had seen better days. He looked about the same age as Jules and Eugene.

'I hope that one at the back isn't in our class at school. He looks a bit mean.'

Peace and quiet returned and they opened the door, carefully so that the string didn't fly in the air. It worked. They hid the string among the leaves and turned back to the river, which was now much calmer, the tide having turned two miles away, where the river met the sea between rocks that dominated that part of the coast. The nearest usable beach was about five miles away, though swimming was not recommended due to strong currents.

After a bit of a struggle, both boys had a fly on their line and attempted to cast into the river. It was not a success. At one time, Jules nearly caught Eugene by the collar, while Eugene caught his hook in a tree. Luckily a short tug released it. They decided just to swing the line out as far as they could and hope for the best.

Soon it was lunchtime and they headed home. They may not have caught a fish, but they now had a den with a door and an unsettling knowledge of the local Moorhead gang.

After lunch Dilys drove Claire and the boys to a large town which sold school uniform and soon both boys were kitted out with everything on the list. It was all getting a bit real and the journey home was much quieter than the outgoing one.

In the morning the boys awoke to the sound of heavy rain on the window and it remained on and off for the rest of the week. The only thing that they could do was to play their indoor games, on or off the computer, alone or together, but always in touch.

Dilys came over for coffee one morning and commented that Eugene had never been so happy and she was glad he had a friend who understood him. Little did she know exactly how adventurous he had become.

The weekend brought the sun back, but Jules was occupied with shopping on Saturday morning in preparation for a visit from his Gran and Auntie Mo, who arrived after lunch. Of course he was pleased to see them, and when he had a chance to speak to Auntie Mo on her own – while his parents made up the spare beds, and Gran had a snooze – he told her about the fishing, the camp and the gang.

'Sounds fantastic,' said Mo, 'Why don't I ask your Mum if I can come and stay at half term for a couple of days, and you can show me everything.'

As soon as the visitors left, late Sunday afternoon, Jules went online, hoping some of his old schoolmates would be willing to talk, but no-one replied. He wanted to show them how good it was in the country, and that he wasn't cut off from the rest of the world.

The next week went by in a flash. The sun shone and the farmers worked all hours to bring in the harvest. Jules and Eugene watched from afar as the machines worked back and forward over the field, throwing up dust. They still didn't catch a fish, but they spent hours scanning the river for the big one. The door to the camp worked a treat, and when the occasional dog-walker passed by above them, they would pull it down and listen until they had passed.

Occasionally a couple would stroll by, arm in arm, or a family out looking for any blackberries that were ripe enough to take home. But all too soon the holiday was over and it would be school the next day. Dad had made a good start in his new job, which paid better than the last so he was able to buy Claire a car of her own. This meant she no longer needed Dilys to drive her into town, though the two women now took it in turns to drive if they were both going on the same day.

Simon – September

Autumn. That's OK. September. The weather's still warm. Good. The first Tuesday in September. Ah! Not so good. Not for Simon, anyway. It was the first day of the new school year, and Simon was not ready to give up his freedom and go back to the classroom.

The summer had been wonderful, with lots of sunshine and plenty to do. Simon's cousins from America had come to stay, and right at this moment would be boarding a plane home.

'Why today?' thought Simon, angrily, 'When I have to go to school!'

How he would have enjoyed going to see them off at the airport, even if it did mean getting up in the middle of the night. He crawled from his bed, opened his curtains, looked up at the vapour trails crossing the clear blue sky and sighed. It was so unfair.

From his window, Simon could see the fields, where they had watched the big harvesting machine, and trees they had climbed. Beyond was the river, edged with bushes where they had made their camps, far away from the adults. Then, just across the bridge he glimpsed the top of the school building and he shuddered.

Why? It was not as if he hated school. In fact, once term was underway he quite enjoyed it – the football, the fun at breaktime and, last year, the rehearsals for the school pantomime. Simon, though still only just eleven, already knew he wanted to be either a famous footballer or a famous actor. He didn't mind which, just as long as he was rich and famous, and could go to the big city in a long, shiny limo.

Simon managed to grunt a few words to his mother over a bowl of cornflakes. He liked cornflakes, he liked his mother, but today he could not raise any enthusiasm for either. He even grunted as he packed his beloved football kit into his bag. He was so fed up – it was just too soon.

Living in a small country village meant Simon was used to his own company during school holidays. Other boys went abroad, or visited exciting relatives in the city or by the sea. Simon's dad was a farmer, so summer holidays were taken up with harvesting. If Easter was late, and lambing over, they might manage a few days with Grandma in Great Yarmouth, but it usually was far too cold and windy to enjoy the seaside at that time of year.

Reluctantly he put on his jacket, hauled his bag onto his shoulder, grunted to Mum and kicked open the door. He paused, took a deep breath and started off down the dust track that passed as a road.

He didn't hurry. He kicked at loose stones, turning his new trainers brown as he imagined himself in midfield for Manchester United, or even Wilford, a local team. Every step reminded him of the wonderful few weeks he had just had. The best holiday ever, and without even having to leave home.

Suddenly he noticed something ahead of him, at the side of the road. He stopped. It looked like a boy. The bright sun made him screw up his eyes. Yes it was definitely a boy. How very strange! The lad was sitting at the side of the road facing the newly-cut cornfield.

Simon drew closer, his shoes crunching on the gravel.

'Good morning!' called the boy without turning his head.

'Not when it's the first day back to school it isn't,' he answered miserably.

Simon noticed the boy, who was probably a little older than himself, was running his hands across the stubble left behind by the harvester.

'My name's Max,' persisted the boy, overlooking Simon's unfriendly answer, 'Isn't it just lovely?'

Simon stopped. He let his bag slip to the floor. Max did not look round but kept on stroking the straw.

'Why are you looking at straw,' asked Simon, sarcastically, 'when there are so many wild flowers over here?'

Simon loved wild flowers and would often sit and sketch them, though never let on to his footie pals.

'I'm not looking,' Max replied, turning himself towards Simon, 'I'm touching.'

Simon looked at Max and gasped. 'I'm sorry, I didn't see ...'

Max laughed. 'That I'm blind, you mean? Funny that you say you didn't see, when you can see.'

Simon wanted to run, even if it meant running to school, just to get away from his embarrassment. Something in Max's laugh stopped him.

'It's all right,' Max insisted, 'I get used to it. I could see once, but I lost my sight in an accident. Now I feel things and try to remember.'

Simon was beginning to like this young man but he was glad Max couldn't see his red face. 'Why are you here?'

'The car broke down. Just across the bridge. Mum sat me down and went to the school for help.

'I don't go to that school,' Max went on, 'I'm going to the new one in town with the special unit for people like me. We're hoping to move into a cottage near here. Keeper's Cottage. Do you know it?'

'I live next door to it!' screeched Simon, realising his life wasn't so bad after all. 'Listen I have to go to school. I can see your Mum coming, I think. I hope you move in. I'm Simon. See you.'

'Yeah, see you,' grinned Max.

Simon ran on to school. Suddenly he could feel the sun, hear the birds and smell the straw. By the time the school bell rang, he was already planning the days ahead, working out where he could take Max, to put some fun into his life, too. He'd be an interesting new mate, he was sure.

Jules and Eugene – new school

The first day at a new school is always daunting. For Jules it was not a problem but Eugene felt a sudden fear of rejection. Maybe he should try not to be so clever – perhaps his old classmates were jealous. Jules was with him, though, so at least he had one friend.

The village school was an old red brick building. There were two entrances, one marked 'boys', the other 'girls', but it soon became apparent that everyone ignored that and used both. As they entered the playground they both wished they hadn't insisted on their Mums staying at home. True they had visited the school in the week before term started, to meet the Head, Mr. Duncan, and their form teacher, Mrs Twinstead, but suddenly they lost confidence.

'Are you OK?' asked a young lad of about their age. 'The bell's gone – we need to go in. Whose class are you in?'

'Mrs Twinstead,' they chorused.

'Me too, come on.'

They followed him over to a line of pupils in the playground and joined on the end. All the class teachers came out holding their registers and once everyone was quiet, led them inside. Once in the classroom, the boy, who introduced himself as Simon, led Jules and Eugene to a table near the window.

'Let's sit here,' he suggested, 'then you can see out. I work best when I can see out over the fields.'

Eugene smiled. He was sure this was one classmate who wouldn't call him a geek.

'Welcome everyone to your new class. Just find a seat if you haven't already. It doesn't matter who sits where for the moment. Just a warning, though, I will split up friends who don't do their work or cause problems for others. Well done Simon Derby. I see you've been looking after our new pupils, Jules and Eugene. Boys I hope you'll be very happy here. Just say if there's anything that's worrying you. It's not a big school so you can't get lost.'

Everyone laughed. Three girls joined them on their table and soon everyone was seated. Folders and A4 lined paper pads were handed out and the register called. Mrs Twinstead then went on to explain what was happening that day.

'As most of you know, I used to teach in the Juniors next door but my main subject, and the one in which I am qualified, is science. I am particularly keen on the subject I will be teaching you this year – Environmental Studies. So when this post was advertised I took the opportunity of applying – and here I am. Today won't be a normal day but I will give you your timetables for the term ahead and proper classes begin after break. Although this afternoon would normally be PSE then Environmental Studies and will be slightly different, hopefully we will have time to talk about what I will be setting you as your project. I have given you your folders so put your names on them.'

The hour remaining to break-time went quickly with a game to help them all remember each other's names. Many had been together in their last class, so Eugene and Jules had the hardest task. Eugene did extremely well and received a round of applause. It was all going very well.

At break-time some of the boys, and a couple of the girls, played football, but Simon led Eugene and Jules over to the courtyard garden where there were benches between raised beds.

'See that girl with the black hair, playing football. She's Billy Moorhead, you don't want to mess with her.'

'Moorhead? Isn't that the gang we saw, Jules?' responded Eugene in sudden panic. This girl sat on the table next to them in class.

'Yeah, she must be the sister of those three brothers.'

'No,' said Simon, 'She has two brothers. She's the third gang member and wears a cap to look like a boy. She's a real sneaky one and Joey, her older brother, he's in Year 9 and has some very nasty mates. It's best to keep clear.'

'I don't remember hearing a Billy when the register was called.' Jules looked for Eugene's nod of agreement.

'Belinda's her real name but everyone except the teachers calls her Billy.'

Simon went on to point out other classmates, with a quick description of each.

'I'm a bit of a loner. A lot of them don't get me. I've been bullied in the past about liking art and wildlife but most of the bullies got bored in the end and started on one of the girls. The Head had a right go at them and made them let me play football with them. Luckily I'm quite good, so they all want me on their team.'

Eugene looked at Jules. 'It'll be me next then.'

'No way. We won't let that happen, will we Simon? Eugene's very clever and great on computers so kids get jealous of him.'

'Just follow my lead, mate, I think we three will be good friends.'

The bell rang and everyone returned to class where the real work began with Maths in Room 5 until lunchtime. The school dinners were really good, not like the old school at all.

Once the afternoon register was called, Mrs Twinstead said 'Listen up everybody, there's no PSE today so we have some time here. We'd like to properly welcome Eugene Miller and Julian Petts to our class. They've just moved in to the new houses across the bridge and I hope you'll make them both very welcome.'

The whole class clapped, especially Simon, who clapped loudest of all.

'Would anyone like to tell us about something they did in the holidays? Yes, Simon, you first.'

Simon took a deep breath. He didn't usually have much to tell, but he was itching to talk about his American cousins and the fun they'd all had together. Eugene nudged Jules when he realised who Simon meant. Several other children followed with their own news. Some had been abroad, others had been to places in England and one had been to Wales.

'Now I'd like to hear from our two new recruits,' said Mrs Twinstead, turning towards them. 'Eugene I'd like you to tell me about Julian please.'

Eugene was a little taken aback, but after a moment's thinking time said, 'Jules is my best mate. His name's really Julian but no-one calls him that except teachers. He lives next door and we both used to live in Densbridge. He's good on the computer and we've both had fun doing our new gardens.'

Eugene couldn't think of anything else to say, so he looked at Jules who shocked him by saying 'Eugene is the cleverest person I know.'

This was not what Eugene had wanted. It was all going to start over again – bullying, having no friends. How could Jules do this to him? Jules, though, had prepared his speech while Eugene had been talking and went on.

'Not everyone is clever enough to realise that being really clever is terrific. My Mum went to school with someone as clever as Eugene and now he's a millionaire. So one day Eugene might be rich and famous too. But that's not why I'm mates with him. And it's not just because he helps me with my maths homework . . . ' The class laughed. '. . . He's a really kind person who would never do anything to upset his mates and I'm so pleased he lives next door to me.'

Eugene's mouth fell open. The whole class clapped wildly. The boy sitting behind Eugene even leaned over and patted him on the back.

'Well,' added Mrs Twinstead, 'what a great recommendation. I'm sure the class will remember my assembly in the Juniors last year when I was teaching my class about talent. We said that everyone has a talent if only they will look for it. Simon's a good artist, I know, and we've seen his pictures in the corridor. Lisa's good at football, I hear. And I'm sure I'll soon learn about all of you and your special skills. Now we're having an extra short break today as the teachers need to have a quick meeting, so off you go.'

Eugene and Jules followed the rest of the class outside. Their classmates were eager to chat and invited them in to their football game. Mrs Twinstead was right. Lisa was brilliant – better than some of the boys. Eugene, who didn't really enjoy sport, decided to have a wander around the grounds. Through a tall iron railing he could see the juniors in their playground next door.

After the bell rang, the class took a trip along to the computer room where they were allowed to look up information that would form the basis of the class project. Eugene, who loved learning about the environment, soon had several pages of notes to take back to class and put into his folder. Mrs Twinstead said they could work in twos or threes, so Jules and Eugene worked with Simon. Each group had until half term to produce a display and folder of notes. They would be placed around the hall for parents' evening at the start of the new half term.

After school the three boys walked together as far as the lane where Simon lived. All three were happy and looking forward to the days ahead.

Once they were alone Eugene said, 'Thanks for the speech earlier.'

'No probs. I just wanted to stop it all starting again.'

Eugene nodded. A new start was just what he needed. Dilys and Claire were waiting for them and relieved that all had gone so well.

Billy Moorhead – nasty piece of work

By the end of the second week, Billy Moorhead had recruited two rather insignificant girls as her gang. Just like her big brother, she ruled the roost. They would block the gangway and make other girls 'ask nicely' to get past.

Billy had also homed in on the fact that Simon's new mates were actually rather clever, and that they were getting ahead on the project while she and her mates spent most of the time avoiding the task. After a couple of weeks, Mrs Twinstead put them on a final warning – produce some good work or split up. Always looking for the easy way out, Billy hatched a plan. Unfortunately for her, another girl at the same table overhead the plan. At break-time she sidled over to the boys and told them, making them swear not to let on who snitched. It seemed the plan was to steal Eugene's folder and take the work as her own.

'What can we do?' Simon asked, knowing the folders weren't locked away.

'Leave it to me,' Eugene said, with a cunning grin on his face.

Next morning they arrived early and asked Mrs Twinstead if they could go in to the classroom early to put away some work Eugene had done at home. Once inside, Eugene passed all his work to the other two to share between their folders. Then he took a wadge of papers from his bag and put them into his folder.

'Mum was making me chuck out some old stuff from our old school. I've put it in my folder plus a couple of sheets I ran off last night. Look.'

The top sheet looked like a genuine piece of project work but the second page read, 'These pages were stolen from Eugene's folder. They are rubbish.'

The folder was placed on top of the pile with the other two at the bottom. Billy's folder was second on the pile.

During break, Billy sneaked into the classroom, removed the papers from Eugene's folder and put them in her own. She didn't have time to read them as she knew she would be in trouble if she was seen.

The next lesson began and Mrs Twinstead asked Billy's group if they'd actually done any work. Billy proudly collected her folder from the shelf and handed it to her teacher. She sat down at her desk and waited for the praise she thought she would get.

Mrs Twinstead read the first page and nodded, but when she turned to the next sheet her features hardened.

'Stand up Belinda. Is this all your own work?'

'Yes, miss, and my mates too. We done really well, 'aven't we?'

The teacher's face reddened. She rose to her feet and thrust the page under Billy's nose. She read it, glared at Eugene and sank down into her seat mouthing 'I'll get you!'

Billy had to eat her lunch next to the teacher on duty and was made to stand outside the Head's door until he had finished his own lunch. She was shocked when her mother arrived and sat on the chair on the other side of the Head's door. When Billy didn't return to class, her two mates said they thought she would be suspended – which turned out to be true. She would not return for a week, during which time she had to work on the project. Her two friends were given the task of making a display based on research and classwork. That would take them to half term.

The weekend which came in the middle of Billy's suspension caused worry for the boys. They knew she would tell big brother Joey and he would not be pleased. They agreed to meet at Simon's house on Saturday. Simon's Mum, who insisted they call her Jennie, welcomed them with home-made lemonade and a slice of currant cake just out of the oven. She was delighted to meet Simon's new friends as he had never brought anyone home before. They seemed respectable and sensible and even more important, into the same things as her son. Eugene asked for water, explaining about his diabetes.

'Would you boys mind running down to Mrs. M's and getting me some more eggs?' asked Jennie. 'Our hens have gone off lay and I know she has some to spare. Here's the money, get me a dozen and be careful how you bring them back. I'll give you a couple of egg boxes and a sturdy bag. See if you can buy Eugene something nice to eat and drink.'

They set off quite happily, but then Simon spotted Joey and Little Mickey Moorhead in the distance. Billy had obviously been grounded by her mother, who was still fuming at losing half a day's work when she was called up to the school. No-one quite knew what Ma Moorhead did for work but she never seemed too hard up.

As the boys pondered on whether to turn back or brazen it out, Simon noticed someone turning out of the lane just ahead of them. It was Max, being pushed by his Mum.

'Max,' called Simon, 'It's me, Simon and my new mates Jules and Eugene. How are you?'

'Good,' replied Max, 'Mum, this is Simon who I told you about.'

At this point, the Moorhead brothers drew level, gave them the evils but moved on.

'I guess they're not mates of yours then. They looked daggers at you.' said Max's Mum.

'We were glad you came by,' said Jules, 'Their sister's in our class and was suspended for stealing Eugene's work.'

'We're just getting some eggs from Mrs. M's then going back to mine,' said Simon, 'Could Max come with us. Maybe he could stay for lunch. Mum won't mind and she could phone you when Max is ready to leave.'

Although Max's house was 'next door' to Simon's, it was actually quite a long way up the road.

Max's mum – whose name was Sally Slater, she told them – agreed on condition they would phone if Jennie said it wasn't convenient. They quickly agreed and Eugene took charge of the wheelchair. He'd had practice with one of his grandparents, and also he was the tallest of the three. Being country lanes there were no kerbs to negotiate, so it wasn't too hard. Sally watched them for a moment, then seeing they could cope, set off on her way. She could now take a shortcut that would not have been possible with the chair and also she could chat more freely with the friend she was visiting. It was always difficult with Max listening in, though he never interrupted or repeated what he'd heard. In fact he was usually engrossed in some game on his special game machine. Sally worried that, although he was popular at school, he couldn't socialise with them easily at weekends.

The eggs collected, the four friends made their way back to Simon's without seeing the Moorheads. Jennie was delighted to meet Max and rang Sally to confirm she was happy to have him there for lunch and asked if he was OK with beef stew and dumplings. Sally arrived at 3pm but stayed for a cup of tea and a natter with Jennie by which time Max had become accepted as part of their crew. They told him about their adventures, the Moorheads and the school project. Despite his blindness, Max was obviously very well educated and was able to make some brilliant suggestions towards their work. They agreed to meet again the following Saturday at Max's, though his time Sally insisted on baking a pie and joining them for lunch, Jennie included.

But who IS Huckleberry Finn?

During lunch the following week, the boys chatted about their adventures so far, the Moorhead Gang and how they'd love to catch the big fish.

'Sounds like Huckleberry Finn, doesn't it Max?' said his mother

At the end of the meal, Jules said he had to go home as his Auntie Mo was arriving soon. The four boys made their way to the front gate, vowing to meet up again soon.

'Just one thing, Max,' Jules asked, 'Just who is Huckleberry Finn?'

Eugene nodded. He'd wanted to ask the same thing. Max laughed.

'It's from a book by Mark Twain that Mum read to me. It's quite old fashioned now but exciting. Twain was one of those people like Oscar Wilde who came out with witty sayings.'

Jules and Eugene weren't sure who Oscar Wilde was but were keen to hear more.

'It's an American story. Huck was a bit of a naughty boy and full of adventures. There's another book about him and his mate Tom Sawyer. But the big differences between them and us are we don't skip school, the Mississippi River is rather bigger than the one here judging from the length of the bridge, and no-one gets killed!'

'Thank goodness for that,' came Simon's response.

Eugene decided to walk back with Jules. They would not see much of each other for a few days so chatted about their next adventure and how they could involve Max. Simon was easy as he could get down in the den with them, but they couldn't get Max down the steps in a wheelchair.

'I'll have a good think about it,' said Eugene and the two parted company, hurrying in to their respective houses as rain began to fall. Typical. Just in time for half-term.

'That you, Jules?' called Claire. 'Well done for getting back in good time.'

She walked into the room and noticed the spots of water on the window pane.

'Oh no, not rain. Just when we've got a visitor coming. I hope we don't get stuck indoors.'

Jules agreed. He wanted to show Auntie Mo the riverbank.

Mo arrived about an hour later, by which time the rain had stopped.

Tea and cakes were brought out and the family sat, half watching the football which Julian had insisted he couldn't miss on the TV, and catching up with all their news.

After tea, Claire and Mo spent a lot of time in the kitchen, so Jules stayed with his Dad in the lounge.

'So son, how are you enjoying Dean's Creek?'

'Great. I was a bit scared at first, but now I think it's fun.'

'And Eugene? Is he now your friend?'

'Yes. He's brilliant. No-one gave him a chance at the old school. Just cos he's clever and doesn't lark around, but really he's just like me. Some of the kids still try to bully him, but Simon and I stand up for him.'

'Well done you. I haven't met Simon yet, have I?'

'No but it would be great if he could come to tea one day, and the others.'

'Others?'

'Max, he's blind and in a wheelchair, and their Mum's, Jennie and Sally. Mum and Dilys would get on well with them. They're cool – and both good cooks.'

'Better not tell your Mum that. You know how she gets in a flap if we have visitors, going through her Mary Berry cookbooks and insisting on watching those baking programmes.'

'Understood,' said Jules knowingly.

Sunday was dry but a bit chilly, so Julian suggested a drive around the area and lunch in a country pub. Jules was itching to get Auntie Mo on her own but realised he'd get his chance when Dad was back at work the next day.

Claire had a broken tooth, so had to go to the emergency dentist, leaving Mo in the care of Jules for the whole of Monday morning.

Eugene ... in trouble

Monday. The first day of half-term and Eugene was bored. It wasn't even mid-morning, but already he was really bored. Jules was with Auntie Mo. He didn't want to meet anyone else. He needed someone who could walk with him in silence and enjoy everything around them without needing to chatter all the time. He could go for a walk alone. Why not? Maybe he'd catch that fish – then Jules would wish he'd been there.

'Don't be too long.' his mother called after him. 'Lunch is at one. I've put a snack in your rucksack for you.'

'Having a diabetic child,' Dilys had told Claire, 'means you always have to watch when and what they eat.'

Eugene's diabetes didn't worry him. He was used to refusing sweets, much preferring savoury snacks, and as long as he had something mid-morning he was fine.

He made straight for the river bank. That's when he saw the fish. It was enormous. He decided to take a shortcut down the bank but slipped. Immediately he knew it was a stupid thing to do. He slipped and slid right into the bushes – the fall felt like a movie in slow motion. His foot caught in the branches but his body didn't stop. The pain in his ankle took his breath away. He tried to dislodge his foot but his weight was pulling him down head first. He was stuck. His fishing rod landed at the edge of the water followed dangerously closely by his mobile phone and emergency sugar supply, both of which escaped from the unfastened side pocket of his rucksack.

He was about to shout for help when he saw the Moorheads on the other bank. He froze. Luckily they were too busy catapulting small birds to notice him.

Keep calm. Keep still. Someone will come by, he thought.

He made several attempts to free himself from the tangled undergrowth that had grabbed his foot but it hurt so much that he decided to try to relax until he could hear someone on the path above. Nobody came. After a while he started to feel dizzy and remembered that in his bad mood he had left his breakfast uneaten in his room. That was not good. He remembered his snack and carefully unfastened the main section of his rucksack. He prised open the packet – not easy upside down. Crackle, crackly. He needed to eat his crisps quietly, in case the Moorheads came back.

Do it quickly. Big noise, short time. He put one small crisp in his mouth. Crunch, crunch. It sounded so loud. He'd never noticed before. But he had to eat.

Cheese and Onion. Why did every multi-pack have to contain Cheese and Onion? But he was hungry. After all it must be about 11 o'clock. He looked at his watch. It had stopped, but as he did so he managed to spill the meagre contents of the crisp packet down onto the water's edge. To add insult to injury, a passing duck waddled ashore and demolished them in seconds. Just one crisp had landed out of reach on a broad leaf and was soon feeding the ants. At least it might stop them trying to crawl up his legs.

His head was swimming. His throat was parched. Why did he forget to refill his water bottle? Stupid mistake. He was too weak now to be cross with himself.

Auntie Mo to the rescue

'Do you like fishing?' Jules asked Mo.

'I haven't done it since I was a kid, but it used to be fun then.'

'I can show you where we fish. There's one big fish but it just won't bite. Come this way along the riverbank.'

They walked the short distance from the bridge to the rise above the fishing patch.

'That's where we see him,' said Jules, pointing out to mid-stream.

'Hush, what's that?' Mo whispered, 'I heard someone moaning.'

'Look,' shouted Jules, 'There's Eugene's phone and rod. Quick, this way.'

They ran along the footpath until they reached the mud steps. Soon both were immediately beneath Eugene. He moaned and they looked up. Jules tried to scramble up to Eugene but the bank was too slippery. Mo was already on her mobile phone.

'I'm not sure, ambulance, no maybe fire brigade. A lad's stuck halfway up a steep bank and he's not looking good,' she was saying.

'He's diabetic, tell them,' prompted Jules.

Mo repeated the information and handed the phone to Jules to give the exact location.

Eugene was vaguely aware of his saviours and allowed himself to drift in and out of consciousness, safe in the knowledge that his ordeal would soon be over.

Just a couple of minutes later a fire engine could be seen by the bridge. Two firemen arrived carrying a ladder and Jules showed them the way down to the fishing patch. Another fireman brought first aid equipment. They soon managed to raise Eugene up, free his foot and then lower him to the ground.

An approaching siren heralded the arrival of the ambulance and once again Jules acted as guide.

'He's diabetic,' Jules told them and immediately they took a sugar reading and gave him what he needed to bring him back into consciousness. Meanwhile Mo rang Dilys who had started to worry when she found the untouched breakfast bowl in Eugene's room.

'You're lucky these people were passing,' said a fireman, 'and that we were just up the road dealing with a small fire next to a barn. That's how we got here so quickly.'

Eugene nodded hazily and managed to smile at Mo and Jules.

At the hospital Eugene was checked over and his parents met him there. An X-ray showed his ankle though badly wrenched was not broken. After two hours of observation and a stern chat from a diabetes nurse about regular meals, he was allowed home with his ankle strapped up.

Jules wanted to go round, but his parents said he should wait until morning. After all, Auntie Mo would be going home early and he would want as much time with her as possible. Jules agreed, but texted Eugene just to let him know he wasn't ignoring him. A smiley face popped up on his phone so he knew all was well.

Mo's visit was over all too soon. As her cab moved slowly out on to the main road, Jules was aware of a knocking sound behind him. He looked up and saw Eugene beckoning to him.

'Just popping in to see Eugene,' he told his Mum and made his way round to the back of Eugene's house. He knew Mrs. Miller would be there, doing her amazing baking.

'Jules,' she said, 'Good to see you. Do go up and see Eugene. He's really much better but we do want him to be completely fit for school.'

Jules climbed the stairs, two at a time, and was soon nattering nineteen to the dozen with his friend.

'I saw it,' whispered Eugene as if someone else was nearby,'The big fish . . . I saw it. That's how I fell. I was taking a short-cut down that overgrown path we saw, but it was slippery from the rain.'

'As soon as you're better, let's go and see if we can catch it – but we'll use the steps!'

'Definitely.'

Bring and eat party
'Mum?' Jules spoke with a question in his voice.

'What are you after now?' Mum replied.

'I've had a brilliant idea.'

'Why does that worry me?'

'No, really. You know how they have Bring and Buy sales at school and everyone brings things and other people buy them.'

'Yes.'

'Well I think we should have a Bring and Eat party. My mates' mums could all come – and Dads if they want – and I could invite Eugene, Max and Simon. You could all make the food, so you don't have to worry about doing it all and we could all eat it.'

'When did you have in mind?'

'Saturday?'

'Sounds like a great idea. Your Dad's going to watch a cricket match so he won't be in until five o'clock but if you ask people to arrive between four and five we can sort out the food. Can you give me the phone numbers for the mums so we don't all bring the same?'

'Yes, great. Thanks Mum.'

Jules wasted no time and soon contacted everyone. Simon's dad said he might be busy on the farm but would try to pop in to meet everyone, but Max's father was working away from home.

By Thursday Eugene was allowed out but on condition that he stuck to paths and didn't go far. Jules met him outside and they strolled along the river path but didn't see the big fish. Suddenly they heard people shouting. It was the Moorheads. Billy was screaming at her brothers but they were laughing and calling her a spoilsport.

Jules and Eugene hid behind a tree, but Billy saw them. They were surprised when she didn't point them out to her brothers and as soon as they were out of sight the boys returned to the path but stood looking into the river. Still no big fish.

Then they saw her. Billy. Running full pelt towards them. She had taken off her cap and her long hair flowed out behind her. There was no time to hide.

'Jules. Eugene. You've got to help me!.'

'Really?' answered Eugene.

'I've left the gang. Things are getting bonkers and I don't want to be sent to prison.'

'Hold on,' said Jules, 'why would you be sent to prison. What have you done?'

'I haven't done anything. It's Joey and Mickey. They started setting fire to things and then watching the fire brigade put them out. They did it the other day outside one of Simon's dad's barns.'

'That must've been the day I had my accident,' Eugene explained.

'Well,' Billy went on, 'they said this time they'd set light to the hay, but that's the animal food for the winter and I love animals. And Simon's OK – he likes animals too – so it would be his dad's animals that might starve.'

'What can we do? You know what they're like.' Jules pointed out.

'We could tell the police,' said Billy.

'Yeh,' said Jules, 'that would put us in danger from your brothers. No I'll ring Simon. His dad will know what to do.'

Jules took his phone from his pocket and very soon Billy was able to talk to Simon's dad who had just dropped in at home for a cuppa. He was very grateful and told them to leave it to him.

Relieved, Jules turned to Billy, 'Where is the barn? Could we hide somewhere and watch what was going on?'

'Yes. My brothers told me which barn. We can sit in the ditch the other side of the field and no-one will see us.'

She led them to the hiding place where the boys took out their snacks. Jules gave Billy some of his crisps. Luckily she had her own water bottle which was slung around her waist on a belt.

Eugene decided he should ring home, just to say he was fine and would explain when he arrived back for lunch. Billy curled her lip, wondering why he had to explain at all.

'He's diabetic.' said Jules, seeing her expression. 'He has to eat regularly or he's ill. His mum worries a lot.'

'Oh. OK. Look there are my brothers, just by the gate over there.'

The brothers looked around, slowly opened the gate and went through, closing the gate behind them. Then Billy pointed to Simon's dad, Paul, behind the barn holding a bucket. The Moorheads couldn't see him from there and crept towards the barn. Paul moved to the side of the barn, being careful not to be seen. Joey struck a match and moved towards the hay. Paul rushed into the barn and threw a bucket of water over the match – and all over Joey. Mickey laughed, Joey hit him, and the brothers tried to run away. Paul called his sheepdog who had been obediently lying in a haycart behind the barn.

'Here boy. Round 'em up.'

Paul gave the dog instructions to circle them to slow their retreat. Billy, down in the ditch with her head behind some grass stalks whispered, 'Look there's a police car. Parking up by the gate and they're going to arrest them. I hope they don't realise I grassed on them.'

'Why would they?' asked Eugene.

'Well just in case,' said Jules, 'Let's run over to the road. Eugene and I will hide and when the police car drives by you can look surprised and shout to them.'

The plan worked. The Moorhead boys looked daggers at Billy but she called out, 'What's happened.' So Joey mouthed 'get Mum'.

'Thank you for helping me. You can come out now. They've gone.'

'Have you really left the gang?' enquired Jules. 'They are bullies.'

'Yeh, so is she sometimes,' was Eugene's almost whispered reaction.

'I think I just wanted to keep up with them. I thought if the family had a bad name I might as well be bad because I'd probably get blamed for everything. My Dad's in prison but before they caught him for stealing a car, the police were always round ours whenever anything went missing.'

'What does your mum say?' asked Eugene.

'Oh she's fed up with him. She does loads of cleaning jobs to get money for our food and stuff. She says she'd leave him but she'd have nowhere to go, and she wouldn't leave us even if we do cause her all sorts of trouble. She'll be well mad when the police call her. I'm not saying anything in case she thinks I was there too. She won't be able to pick them up until after six today because she's doing a big half-term clean at the school.'

'Serves them right,' the boys chorused.

'Could I be in your gang now?'

'We aren't a gang.' Jules insisted, 'and I'm not sure we want a girl hanging around.'

'But I'm tough. I've been dressing like a boy and keeping up with Mickey and Joe, so you wouldn't always have to be helping me.'

'We'll think about it. And we have to ask Simon, and Max – he's our blind friend.'

'OK,' added Eugene, 'We'll let you know at school on Monday.'

Billy grinned and ran off back to the bridge and home for lunch. As the boys strolled to their houses Eugene pointed out that he'd said Monday because he didn't think they wanted her at the Bring and Eat Party.

'No way! My mum wouldn't want her mum there either.'

It started to rain so they walked faster – Eugene still had pain in his ankle so didn't want to run. By the time they reached The Close, it was raining hard so they arranged to meet in Eugene's room as soon as they'd had lunch to have a go on his new game.

Both boys told their parents about the morning's events but asked them never to tell anyone they were involved. Billy had said her brothers would go to prison, but they were too young for that, though they did have to go to court and were given a stern warning that if they were caught again it would be worse for them.

Billy, being the good little actress that she was, managed to convince her family that she was nowhere near. But she did say she didn't want to go round with them. She never went back to find her cap and was happy to let her hair hang loose or put it in bunches.

Party time

The four mums had been in touch and divvied out the catering for the party. Sally suggested they have the party on her lawn behind Keeper's Cottage and Claire agreed as theirs had only just been laid and wasn't very big.

Jennie suggested that she should bring cheeses and cold meats from their own produce. She explained it was all processed in Granfold and distributed to their customers with a small amount kept back for their own use. Dilys would make bread rolls and buy some extras items for Eugene. Sally would make a cake and some biscuits and Claire would provide drinks and some of her Mary Berry scones. It sounded like an awful lot of food, but the party was to start at lunchtime and continue until tea-time.

Saturday came, and by mid-day they had all assembled at Keeper's Cottage. While Max took the boys to what he called his suite – a bedroom with its own shower room and loo – the mums began sorting the food, plates and cutlery. Jennie asked if she could put together a few things for Paul who dropped in during a short break from working in the field nearby. Having met everyone and collected his packed lunch he headed off, calling back that he'd be working late.

'Come on boys.' called Sally, 'Take these rugs and spread them on the lawn please, Simon. Max, let me put your tray on your chair and you can take out the plates and things. You two go and help bring the food out. Thanks.'

When Dilys complimented her on the way she organised the boys, Sally told them she'd been in the army. That was how she had met Jim, Max's Dad.

'He works for an IT company and now travels all over the world., but back then he was based in Salisbury and so was I. Once I had Max, I decided to take an office job in Jim's firm rather than being posted all over the place. Jim kept getting promoted, so ironically it's him who now has to spend weeks abroad, but I don't mind. It keeps our marriage fresh.'

Sally passed round the plates and made up a roll for Max.

'Max loves cheese and pickle sandwiches, Jennie, so with your cheese and this lovely pickle you've definitely made a fan.'

'Well actually I make a big batch from our apples and tomatoes and sell them to the village shop. I'll send a jar over for you as a moving in gift.'

'Thanks. Now tuck in everyone. There's plenty and what we don't eat now we'll put out again for tea.'

The afternoon passed pleasantly. Dilys brought out an old miniature croquet set and soon they were all competing for the championship. Jules gave a running commentary for Max who seemed to be enjoying the fun. Eugene was just doing a lap of honour, pretending to hold a cup above his head when he stopped short.

'Oh no,' he muttered.

Everyone looked towards the field behind the garden. Billy was strolling through, hands thrust deep in her pockets and a pony tail swinging out behind her.

'Hi guys! So this is where your mate lives. I wondered where you'd got to.'

'Whose your friend?' asked Dilys.

The way Jules looked at her immediately told her she had said the wrong thing.

'Have you decided if I can join your . . . you know?'

'Not yet Billy,' said Jules, 'We need to ask the others, so we'll do that in a bit. See you at school. Oh, and you're not supposed to come round here, it's private.'

'OK, see yas.'

'Not a friend then,' laughed Dilys, 'I was just about to invite her in when I saw the look on your face.'

'She's the sister of those trouble-makers I told you about,' said Eugene, 'She says she doesn't want to do bad things any more and wants to join us. She thought we were a gang, but we're not. She's quite tough for a girl, and can be a good laugh, so maybe we'll give her a chance.'

The Mums all started giving warnings about gangs but the boys said they would only take her in with them if she could prove she really had left the gang. After they had all eaten the leftovers and the Mums had gone into the kitchen to wash up, Max brought up the subject of Billy.

'I don't mind that she's a girl but I think you should be careful to start with. Don't show her your den or tell her about the big fish. Not until she's proved herself.'

Simon, who had been quiet up until then said, 'OK, we'll talk to her at school and make some rules. We could say we're a club and she's not allowed to join for a month. By then we can see if she's been tempted to go back with her brothers.'

'Or if they've bullied her into it,' added Eugene.

So it was agreed, and Billy was told at school on Monday. At first she was a bit miffed not to be accepted straight away, but she had to admit she could see their reasons. She did suggest she might stop being called 'Billy', but the boys thought it suited her. And besides everyone called her Billy – even some of the teachers.

The River Club

For four days it rained most of the time, so it wasn't until Friday that outdoor breaktime was resumed. Billy had worked very hard in class, trying to show she'd stopped her old ways. Her former girlfriends no longer spoke to her, but without her leadership, even their behaviour improved slightly.

It was Simon who started the conversation about the coming weekend. Not wanting to draw attention to the den and their special part of the river, he suggested they meet at the bridge and decide what to do. They all agreed, and Eugene phoned to let Max know the plan.

Saturday turned out to be warm and the wind dropped. Max parked himself on the path at the end of the bridge and said goodbye to his mother, promising to be back in time for lunch. Once all five were assembled Jules suggested they should be a club, rather than a gang, and everyone put in their suggestions for names.

'Listen,' interrupted Max, 'what can you hear. The tide is coming up the river, I think. Let's be *The River Club*. We can call ourselves The Rivs, for short.'

All agreed and various ideas were put forward about secret passwords and so on, but suddenly the peace was shattered. A large estate car drew up and out spilled a family of six, armed with picnic bags, cans and bottles. They narrowly avoided knocking into Max's chair as they made their way down the stone steps and on to a flat area beside the river.

'Let's go somewhere else,' suggested Eugene not waiting for an answer and skilfully pushing Max over to the far side of the bridge. The others followed. There was a bus shelter a short way off and as the sun was now beating down on them, they went in and sat on the bench. Nobody could think of something to do, especially with Max being in the chair. He explained that he was having physio and could now manage a few steps with a walking frame, but he would never walk properly.

While Eugene ate his snack, the others each told their story, with Jules explaining how he and Eugene arrived in Dean's Creek and became friends. Max explained how he had been hit by a car and had brain damage which took away his sight and his ability to walk. At first his parents were told he had only a small chance of survival, but then he woke up. He couldn't speak but had to work hard to regain his ability to talk. Even now he had a slight slur in his voice and he would forget words, but it was barely noticeable. He had been having physio to build up his strength, and now his arm muscles were strong they wanted him to try a walking frame. His legs were not able to support him without one. Billy listened and sat in silence.

Simon was next to tell his story.

'Not much to tell. I've always lived here and my Dad's a farmer. Mum's an artist – that's how I learned to draw. Both my parents know all about the countryside so now I do too.'

'You're so lucky,' Billy moaned. 'All my parents know about is thieving and fiddling the benefits. They both left school without taking exams – probably kicked out I should think. My brothers are just following their ways, but I hate it. I want to pass my exams and move out as soon as I can. I didn't realise that until I saw you guys enjoying the school project. You can teach me about the plants and animals if you like.'

'Sounds like a plan,' said Jules, 'but it's time to get Max home and then we have to go in for lunch. Let's meet up here at two.'

Billy agreed and wandered off along the river bank to the tatty run-down building she called home. No-one was in, so she made a sandwich and a cup of tea and sat down in front of the television until it was time to return to the bus shelter.

On the way to Max's place, the boys chatted about Billy's sad story and agreed to give her a chance. Sally greeted them, saying she was going to visit a friend after lunch so would take Max to the meeting point for two o'clock.

After lunch Eugene grabbed a notepad and pencil from his drawer before calling for Jules. Once the Club was assembled Eugene handed the pencil and pad to Billy.

'We're going to start teaching you about the countryside, and you won't remember it all at first, so make some notes, scribble some quick sketches, whatever helps.'

'You're all so kind to me,' said Billy, as she pretended the tear that sprang to her eye was just a bit of grit. 'I feel so bad about the way I was when we first met.'

'It's what you do in future that counts,' said the ever-wise Max.

Simon suggested they take a stroll across the bridge and along the river path where there were lots of wild flowers and birds to identify. Once across the bridge Simon let out a little shriek.

'Look, down there. That family left all their rubbish behind. They even left the carrier bag they brought, so why couldn't they just fill it up and take it away. Flippin' townies!'

Jules and Eugene exchanged a smile. They had been townies themselves until August but they would never leave such a mess. Billy ran down the steps and grabbed the bag.

'Come on. Help me. We can soon get it cleared up.'

It took less than two minutes to bag up the rubbish. The local policeman stopped by the bridge and looked down.

'Good to see someone actually taking their rubbish home,' he called.

'It's not their rubbish,' explained Max, 'Some townies had a picnic, but they're clearing it up.'

'Well done lads . . . and . . . oh, Billy Moorhead. What a surprise.'

'I'm going to be good from now on,' she called back.

'Glad to hear it. Keep it up.' And off he cycled, wondering how this miracle could have happened.

Billy carried the full bag up to the road and pushed it into the litter bin.

'Not as if they had far to carry it, is it?' Jules muttered.

'My Mum's got one of those grabber things in the shed,' said Billy suddenly. 'Like the park-keeper uses. She never uses it now. I think she got it for stealing peaches off our neighbour's tree. He caught her one day and put up a wall with spikes on it so she had to stop. If I find it, we could go litter picking around the village.'

'I can bring some black sacks,' added Eugene. 'We could keep them in the d . . . .'

He stopped suddenly, realising he'd given the game away. Billy had guessed.

'You've got a den? Really? Show me. I mean please show me. I won't tell anyone.'

Simon looked at the others then shrugged. 'Well we were going to wait until you joined the Club properly, but I do think you've changed. What do you think guys?'

They all agreed but said if she told anyone about the den they'd never speak to her again.

Of course, Billy was delighted and promised faithfully, on her life, that it would be their secret. So off they all went along the river path to the makeshift steps.

'I can't see a den. It's just a bit of riverbank,' complained Billy.

Then Jules untied the branch that covered the entrance and she gasped in amazement. They heard voices. Billy immediately recognised her brothers' usual shouts and pulled the boys into the den.

Eugene pulled the branches down and Max, who had been waiting up on the path, heard them and carefully wheeled himself further along, feeling the bushes on the side furthest from the river to keep safe, so that he was well away from the den.

'This is great,' whispered Billy.

On the other bank, Joey grabbed Mickey's cap and threw it into the river, shouting that it served him right for arguing. Mickey, knowing he'd be in trouble with their Mum, started to cry. Joey called him a baby and ran ahead and up to the bridge. Mickey looked down at his cap, floating along just too far out to reach, then reluctantly went to catch up with his brother.

'He's in big trouble,' Billy confirmed. 'Mum'll thrash him.'

They left the den, closing it safely and rejoined Max who had heard it all.

'Billy,' Eugene said after a while, 'can you run home and get that grabber? We might be able to get Mickey's cap if we go round to the other bank. Can you see it?'

'It's caught up on some weed, so it might not move,' added Jules.

Billy didn't need to be asked twice. She ran off, agreeing to meet them on the far bank. On her return she found the boys had gathered up some wooden boards that had been dumped on the bank and were making a sort of jetty out towards the weed bed. Billy was easily able to walk along it and retrieve the cap. It was a bit muddy, so she quickly rinsed it in the river, wrung it out and gave it a good shake. They rejoined Max, who was waiting on the bridge,

'Now what?' asked Eugene.

No-one had a plan as to how Billy could give the cap back to Mickey without suspicion. Jules suggested they take the boards round to the den in case they were of use in the future.

'I know,' suggested Simon. 'Leave the grabber with me and take the cap home. Put it on Mickey's bed and come back to the den.'

The boys were just pushing the boards into the den when they realised Joey was on the bridge and about to head home. They also also spotted Max's mother on the bridge and he asked Eugene to push him to meet her so she could take him home.

The other two hid and Joey strolled on without seeing them. They heard him shout 'dirty traitor' to Billy who started to run towards the bridge. Joey laughed but didn't follow. Then Mickey appeared and headed towards home.

As he passed Billy she called out, 'Look on your bed. You owe me now!'

Once both brothers were safely out of sight Billy rejoined Jules and Simon.

'Have I passed the test?' she asked.

'We'll see,' said Jules. But secretly he knew she could now be trusted.

The Project in danger

November brought high winds and a lot of rain, so whereas the boys were all now keeping in contact on line at weekends, Billy felt left out. She was given a computer to use by the school, but said she wouldn't take it home as her brother Joey would take it. Instead homework was done at Homework Club after school. Sometimes, if she was working on the project, the boys would stay behind with her. They hardly saw Max in person but he was pleased to keep in touch.

One Saturday, Jules and Eugene went to check on the den. It was still in place, but with leaves falling from the trees, it didn't give much cover.

'Look,' shouted Eugene suddenly, 'over there. It's the huge fish. Typical when we didn't bring our rods.'

'It's amazing,' agreed Jules, 'but it seems a pity to catch it. It must be quite old.'

Eugene pulled out his new phone and took a picture just in time, as the fish suddenly turned and swam away.

'So good that we actually saw it though,' he said, slipping his phone safely into his pocket.

On their way home, they passed the old lady who had told them about the fish. What were the chances of that on the very day it had shown itself?

The old lady was delighted and said it was a sign of good luck to come. Her husband had always told her he had good luck whenever he saw it. One time they won ten pounds on the lottery.

Eugene didn't have time for superstition, but Jules secretly hoped something good would happen.

Once home they went to Eugene's room to play a game until lunchtime. Dilys brought them a drink and snack, and instead of just going back downstairs, she sat on the end of the bed.

'I've just had a call from Max's mum. It's his birthday on Friday, and she's giving him a surprise party on Saturday. She wants you two to come and bring Billy and Simon. There will be a couple of his schoolfriends and his cousin Ellie. She's ten and is staying with them for the weekend. Good thing really, as Billy would be the only girl.'

'That probably wouldn't bother her,' Jules assured her, 'It's probably that she'd be company for Ellie.'

'Sally has got him some special computer games Max wants, so the plan is we buy them between the four of you and surprise him with them.'

'I don't think Billy has any money,' Eugene pointed out.

'Never mind. We'll put her name on them anyway,' Dilys said, gathering up the empty cups and heading back downstairs.

Back in school at break time, the boys told Billy the plan, not mentioning anything about money. But Billy quickly realised she should contribute, so offered to see if they had some wrapping paper in what she called Mum's stash in the loft. She didn't think it wise to mention that it was probably part of one of her mother's shoplifting sprees.

They had been standing by the wall between the tarmac playground and the field and had no idea that Joey was listening to every word on the far side of the wall.

Suddenly he appeared. 'OK, so where's the party?'

'You're not invited,' shouted Billy.

'I'll tell Mum you're nicking her paper.'

'So I'll ask her first!'

'Tell me where the party is or I'll make you sorry.'

The bell rang and Joey left them with a glare. The boys told Billy not to say anything, but she had no intention of spoiling things for Max. But she was worried about how Joey would get her back for keeping the secret.

That afternoon Billy went to the homework room to do her maths. She was just about to pack up and leave when Mickey came rushing into the room carrying her project folder. Miss Gibbs, the staff member in charge that day was astonished to see someone from the lower school coming in in such a state.

'Take it Billy,' Mickey yelled. 'Joey was going to rip it up. Good job Mum was in your room changing the bed, cos he would've. I went in when he was in the loo and told Mum you needed it for homework club . . . and . . . here it is.'

Miss Gibbs grasped the situation, thanked Mickey and agreed to keep the project folder in her cupboard until morning, when Billy could retrieve it and arrange for it to be kept permanently in her own classroom.

As Billy and her little brother headed home, Mickey said, 'That's for getting my cap out of the river. Now we're even.'

Next morning Billy explained to the boys and their teacher that the project had nearly been destroyed but begged them all not to say anything to Joey. He was still angry about the party but luckily someone his family called 'Uncle Bob' – even though he was no relation – had managed to get tickets to a football match on Saturday. He asked Joey if he wanted to go with him, so the party was soon forgotten.

Friday was wet and gloomy and although Max had a new console from his parents, he had to head off to school before the post came. Even when he arrived home and his mum helped open his cards everything seemed a bit boring. He hadn't told his mates it was his birthday, so didn't expect any messages.

His relatives arrived and gave him their presents, most of which were edible. The adults were all busy chatting and catching up on news, so he was left to entertain Ellie who insisted they do a kind of jigsaw designed for sight impaired people she had bought him. It was quite a complicated one, so she soon lost interest and went to watch television leaving Max with a large board across the table of his wheelchair. His uncle came to the rescue and put the board in a safe place.

Once everyone had finally gone to bed, Max lay there, wondering what the world held for a boy who was now a teenager, was blind and needed to be pushed everywhere.

Max's surprise

Next morning Max was aware of a lot of bustling about in the kitchen. His mother had been in there with his aunt for a couple of hours after breakfast, making the excuse that they had a lot of nattering to catch up on. Uncle John suggested he help Max with the puzzle as Ellie was skipping in the garden.

When lunch was served everything seemed to calm down. Sally had made fish cakes and salad followed by fresh fruit salad. Max presumed it was a light meal because Auntie Kate was on one of her diets. Just two hours later he was to find out the real reason.

At around 3pm he heard the front door open. Strange. Everyone was inside and he was sure the person had used a key. Dad! It must be Dad.

'Hi son,' called Jim, 'Happy Birthday. I only have a few hours between flights but I had to come to see you. I've finished my work in India and have to fly to The States to sort out the paperwork and so on, but the best news is that I'll be working in London next month.'

'That's the best birthday present,' shouted Max, giving his Dad the biggest hug.

Max had only just finished opening his presents from Jim when the door bell rang. In came his mates, the entire River Club with cards and his gift, which Max described as 'perfect'. They were introduced to Jim and soon there was so much chatter going on that Max's head was absolutely buzzing.

Sally and Kate busied themselves with party food which they brought into the dining room to make space in the kitchen, while Ellie dragged Billy into the garden to 'do skipping'.

Max's gloom from the previous day had disappeared, and although his future was still a big question mark, he knew he had the love of his family and friends, and that meant a lot.

By six, everyone had left apart from Jim, giving the family some time together before Jim's cab arrived to take him to the airport. Max slept better that night than he had for ages.

Class challenge

Being a church school, morning assembly was part of the school day that was not negotiable. Not that it was any great hardship – just a hymn, prayers and announcements – but it always happened without fail. So when Mrs Twinstead announced on Monday morning that assembly was cancelled, everyone was shocked.

'The Head has sent out a challenge. As you know, next Monday is Parents' Evening and we want to show your parents how well you've done so far this year. I mentioned some while ago that your projects would form part of a display, and now you will need to complete your group presentations by Friday lunchtime when the Governors will come in and judge them. There is a prize for the best class. Then parents will have the chance to see them and vote for the best group project within that class. The winning group will also receive a prize. You will be able to complete your displays during my lesson, lunch breaks and any wet breaks plus after school on Tuesday and Thursday when I will be here to supervise you.'

Billy's group, none of whom were now talking to each other, looked decidedly miffed. Although they'd had a head start on the display aspect during Billy's absence, the other two in her group had fallen out over a boyfriend and much of the later work was individual rather than group work. However, they decided they'd at least try to win.

Simon had great ideas for their display, and Eugene had researched their area thoroughly and found a lot of information about the history of the village, its wildlife and environmental aspects. Jules typed up Eugene's notes putting the information into everyday language where it was rather technical. His Dad had helped him unpick some of the jargon he did not understand and Simon's Dad had found some old photos of the farm so Jules could include them within the text. In fact the whole class had worked very hard. One group had looked at the river and how it had changed over the past century while another investigated the impact of industry in the nearby large town.

Billy had persuaded her group to look at the wild flowers, using the knowledge she had gained from the boys.

Group member Mina borrowed her mum's flower press. They only took one example of each flower, knowing some might be rare. The third group member, Emily, was the artistic one so she constructed the back drop for the display. Despite their internal feud, the group actually managed a good bit of team work. Their wasn't a lot of written work, but it looked great.

By Friday morning all classes had their displays up and ready. Mrs Twinstead's classroom was not going to be used by any class but hers so she allowed the pupils to put any display that would stand up unsupported on tables in the middle of the room while others adorned the walls. It looked like an environmental grotto. The cleaner commented that evening that she'd taken twice as long sweeping the floor as she didn't want to knock anything over.

On Monday the normal timetable was cancelled to avoid spoiling any class displays. The day began with an extra long assembly, with the Head talking about Parents' Evening first.

'Please ask your parents to come promptly at the arranged times. Remember teachers have homes to go to and some live quite a way from the village, so it would be a shame to keep them here late. Some of you have been asked to act as guides for the areas where teachers will be talking to your parents. I have also appointed one classroom assistant for each classroom so that your displays are guarded at all times. We don't want any mindless vandalism like last year.'

Everyone who had been in the school before this year knew he was talking about Joey. Billy was too embarrassed to tell any of the newcomers it was her brother who sabotaged some of the better work. Luckily she also knew he was not going to be around that evening as he and his mates were planning to steal booze from the local pub.

The landlord was a parent, so would leave someone else in charge – and that someone was not a big tough guy like Mr Bridges himself.

'Finally,' said the Head, at last, 'The winning class has been chosen by the Governors and they will go on a school outing to the new theme park that has just opened down by the coast.'

There was an excited murmur across the hall. Everyone hoped their class would win.

'It wasn't easy to choose, especially as every year group has a different area of the environment to cover. Our new intake just centred on the local area, with older years spreading outward to the county, the country and then the world. But a winner we have, so very well done and let's have a big round of applause for Mrs Twinstead's class. Their display will be brought to this hall after Parents' Evening and placed on the stage for all to see.'

There was applause, though a little half-hearted as other classes realised they hadn't won.

The winning class clapped and whooped with excitement.

'Now off to break all of you and you all know where you should be afterwards, though some may be in different areas to usual for today.'

At afternoon registration Mrs Twinstead congratulated her class and reminded them that parents would be touring the school then voting for the best project in her class .

It was obvious that parents would vote for their own children, but parents with children in other classes would vote on merit. Mrs Duncan, the Head's wife, was already assigned to whichever class won, as the couple lived next door to the school. It didn't matter that they would be last to leave, so she would supervise the voting and count up at the end. The caretaker was to be given the evening off so he could go to the pub with his mates, and the Head would check the building and lock up.

Crime doesn't pay

Stubbs the caretaker was just leaving his house for a much anticipated booze-up with his mates when he noticed Joey and another boy from year nine standing on the pavement outside. He waited with his door slightly open in order to hear the conversation. Soon they were joined by two ex-pupils, both now 18 years of age.

'So you know what to do,' Joey was saying, 'You two go in and order a drink, then you Olly go through to the loo, unlock the backdoor and let us in. When we've taken as much as we can carry between us, we'll come to the door and call you. We'll just say someone wants you for something.'

'Yeh,' Olly agreed, 'then we carry the stuff back to my place and get ready to party on Saturday.'

Stubbs waited until they had moved off, then rang the police. He also rang the pub and warned the two women running the bar that night, suggesting they could take their time serving the two young men. Then he went there himself and met his mates.

'There's a pint here for you,' said one of his pals. 'Barmaid says it's on the house. How did you manage that?'

Stubbs just grinned and tapped the side of his nose with his finger.

As soon as the two lads were served and the barmaid turned away to serve another customer, Olly made his way to the toilets. He returned quickly so that he wouldn't be missed. Ten minutes passed. The two looked anxious. Something was wrong. A phone rang and one of them pulled it from his pocket, looked at his mate, then answered it.

'What do you mean it's locked? I unlocked it.' he whispered. Then after a pause continued. 'Cellar door? No. I didn't know that would be locked. It isn't usually. . . . No I don't know. Hold on.'

Olly turned to his mate. 'You go this time. Help them force the door open.'

Five minutes later he returned, nodding his head.

Then it all kicked off. There was shouting from the corridor. The lads in the bar decided to make a getaway but were confronted by two police officers who escorted them into the corridor. There more police were arresting Joey and his pal. Soon all of them were on their way to the police station. Someone at the station pointed out that the two minors would need a responsible adult there.

'Well I don't know who we'd find for Joey,' joked the desk sergeant, but P.C. Webb was called up in his car and asked to go to fetch Joey's mother as she was not contactable by phone.

Joey was furious. Not only had his plan failed, but now they were insulting his mother. He turned and thumped one of the officers, knocking him to the ground. Joey was marched off to a cell.

When P.C. Webb arrived at the house, Josie Moorhead was still on the phone. He knocked on the door.

'Mickey,' she yelled, 'get the door, it's probably that customer back for the watch.'

'Gotta go,' said Josie, ending the call as she saw who was entering her living room. There, all around her and plain to see were items from a local burglary and numerous other valuables she had stolen from shops.

'Well, Mrs. Moorhead,' said PC Webb, looking like the cat that got the cream. 'I was going to take you to the station because your Joey's been arrested, but I think maybe some of my colleagues had better come and talk to you about this little lot first.'

He noted that Billy was in the house, and suggested she take Mickey upstairs and look after him. He walked out on to the front step and called the station. Josie, meanwhile, in panic, crept into the hallway, picked up the baseball bat she kept behind the door curtain and belted Webb over the head. As he fell she pushed past him, calling up to Billy to be good and look after Mickey. Then she ran up the lane and into the nearby woods.

Billy called an ambulance and told them what had happened. The police helicopter sighted Josie with infra-red cameras and soon she too was on her way to the police station. P.C. Webb was taken away in an ambulance and a woman called Mrs Jacobs came to 'sort out' the children.

'Well I'd call that a good night's work if it weren't for the injuries sustained by two of our chaps,' said the desk sergeant.

A good home

Mrs Jacobs helped Billy and Mickey pack a bag each and drove them about five miles to a temporary foster home with a lady called Dolores who was very kind and welcoming, but who explained she only took emergency cases, so as soon as permanent foster parents could be found, she would have to say goodbye to them.

For the rest of the week, the two of them had to be taken to school by taxi, which only enhanced Billy's embarrassment. Everyone knew her mother and brother had been arrested. However, in assembly the Head asked for understanding. He said Billy had become a model student since she distanced herself from her brothers and right now needed all the friends she could get. Billy felt a tear in her eye, but she knew he had meant well.

She dreaded going out to break, but in fact lots of her year group, and those who knew and disliked Joey, came over to tell her how lucky she was to get away from him. Billy felt better.

Simon, Jules and Eugene assured her she would still be a member of the River Club, even if she had to move away permanently. This was not a great comfort to Billy but at least it made her feel wanted.

It was Saturday when Billy and Mickey were driven back to the village and taken to Mrs M's shop. On arrival Mrs M greeted them warmly and took them into the back room. What she said next astonished them.

'Well my dears, everything has come together nicely. You see, nobody knew except my family, but I had a million pound lottery win. You probably noticed that Stonebridge Manor was being done up. Well I bought it so that I could fulfil my lifelong ambition to foster children. I'm moving in this week, and by next weekend you will be able to join me.'

'Wow!' cried Mickey

'You will stay with Dolores Brown until then, but Social Services have said you won't be going back to live in your own home for a long time.'

'Never would be soon enough,' muttered Billy.

'You will each have your own room and can make them like home. At first you will have the bedding I brought from here but we will go out and choose what you would like – two sets each. It's all so exciting – I didn't expect it to happen so fast.'

At that moment the shop doorbell tinkled and Mrs M went in to serve. Billy recognised the voice as Simon's and rushed into the shop gabbling on at nineteen to the dozen about their good luck. Mrs M smiled. She was pleased Billy had accepted her so quickly. Simon paid for his goods and told Billy to tell him the rest at school before rushing off to meet the others at the river bank as they had arranged.

'She's a quiet one,' exclaimed Jules, 'Who would have guessed she'd won the lottery?'

'That explains it though,' added Max.

'Of course,' said Eugene, patting Max on the back. 'Your Mum and mine are going to be running the shop. I thought Mrs M was a bit young to be retiring.'

Two days before the move, Mrs Twinstead's class went on their prize outing. Despite the chilly weather they all had a fantastic time. Some of the parents came along to help and soon everyone was agreeing that it had been worth all the hard work on their projects. On the Friday, in assembly, the Head announced the individual group winners.

'I'm particularly proud of this group,' he began. 'Two of them have only been in the village since August, yet they already know more about its environment than I do.'

Jules and Eugene looked at each other in astonishment.

'Yes it is you Jules and Eugene, along with Simon. Well done to you. Please come to my room at break to collect your prize.'

The next hour dragged by. All the boys had tried to guess what they would get. Book tokens? Pen sets, maybe?

The reality was much better. One adult and one child ticket each to the new James Bond film that had just opened in the nearest big cinema. On arriving home, each of them was surprised to find out that their parents already knew. Mrs Twinstead had sounded them out to see if that's what they would like, and the booking had been made for Saturday. As Billy was moving that day, she wouldn't feel left out.

Billy and Mickey were driven back to their home just long enough to gather up their most precious and essential belongings before being taken to Stonebridge Manor. It was Mrs Jacobs who took them and on arrival she ushered them into the lounge where they all sat on the gorgeous comfy chairs.

'Now then you two. This is a new venture for Mrs May so I want you to be as helpful as you can. Billy I know, from what I've heard through your teacher, that you've turned over a new leaf and stopped doing bad things. That's one reason why I've kept you in the village close to your new friends. Mickey. I think you were easily led by Joey and just followed his lead.'

Mickey looked down at his feet.

'I don't think you are a bad boy and if you follow your sister, I'm sure you will do just fine.'

'I don't have to go round with him though do I?' asked Billy, horrified that she'd be lumbered with her little brother.

'No. But keep an eye on him. He will still have his friends from school and I've already spoken to a couple of Mums who say he's actually very polite and well behaved whenever they've allowed him to play with their boys.'

'So he will have his own social life,' added Mrs M, coming in with glasses of home-made lemonade and slices of her ginger cake, 'and those boys and other friends will be welcome to come here any time. There's an outbuilding which I'm turning into a den for the purpose. You can help me with what to put in it.'

It was all going so well that Billy was afraid she was dreaming. Mickey hoped his mother, who had never paid him any attention, would be locked up for a long time.

'Do we still call you Mrs M', asked Billy.

'Why not? Everyone does. It's better than my first name which I never did like. It's Agatha. My mother was a big fan of Agatha Christie you see.'

They didn't, but they did think Agatha was an unsuitable name for Mrs M.

Christmas Break

On the last day of term, Mrs Twinstead had three boxes of chocolate biscuits on her desk at registration – and they weren't ones she'd been given.

'I expect you're wondering why I have biscuits here. Well I decided there were three girls in this class who had worked very hard after a bad start. Billy, Mina and Emily, these are for you. Don't eat them in school, try to save them for Christmas if you can. I'm very proud of you, and just for the record, I know you fell out over something unimportant . . . '

Those in the class who knew it was about a boy sniggered.

' . . . but you've made up now, and let me tell you this, I have a couple of schoolfriends who I still meet up with even now and they are the best friends I could wish for.'

The girls stepped forward to receive their gifts, each one grinning from ear to ear. They didn't think they would stay mates forever, although Mina and Emily were more likely to than Billy. She was happy with the River Club.

Everyone was occupied with their own families over Christmas. Mrs M gave Billy, Mickey and another two foster children the best time she could and had a big New Year party for them and their friends. She said she hoped to have lots more children there over the next year to make her dream come true. Max raised his glass of lemonade and said, 'Here's to Mrs M!' and everyone clapped.

The new Mickey

On the day after the party, Billy found Mickey in her room, looking at her project. Mina and Emily had agreed she could keep it as she'd done most of the work. She was about to get cross with him but he started asking her sensible questions about the pictures, so she sat with him for a while.

Later she phoned Jules and told him.

'Would you let Mickey look at your project Jules? He's really interested in mine, and I think it might give him a new interest.'

'Why not? I think that's great,' said Jules whose turn it was to have their project at home.

Next day, Billy took Mickey over to Jules's house and Eugene joined them. Mickey was really interested, so it was agreed he could go with them on some of their walks, although each of them knew the den would be out of bounds until he'd proved himself. They worried Joey might still come back and start leading him astray but once they knew he was locked away in a young offenders 'home' for a good long time, and his mother in prison also for even longer, they did decide Mickey could become part of the Club.

The weather was pretty dreadful through January, and the snow in February tended to lend itself to a new type of entertainment. Max was away for a few weeks at a specialist hospital where he was to have intensive physiotherapy to help him stand and walk a little better. He had already made progress at the local hospital and could at least stand and transfer to an armchair which was a great help to Sally. He was getting too heavy for her to manage and the more he moved about the better able he would be to keep his weight down.

So it was March before the friends met up again at the bus shelter. Max told them he could now walk a few yards with a frame as the feeling was coming back to his legs. He never talked about his accident except to say he had been hit by a car and had injuries to his back and head. It seemed from what Sally had told Claire and Dilys, that the nerves were slowly mending but no-one knew how much movement Max would ever manage. He'd also spent a day at the eye hospital in London.

With his Dad now working in London, he wasn't so free to join the others at weekends when Jim stayed overnight and wanted to take Max and Sally out or just spend time with them. Not feeling they had to tailor their activities to Max's limitations meant the River Club members could spend more time on the riverbank. At other times they worked in Mrs M's garden – a job they really enjoyed and for which they received pocket money. The garden was a real nature reserve and once all the unwanted brambles, nettles and weeds were tamed it was a wonderful place to watch birds.

Nobody knew what was in the flower beds until something popped up. Mickey took special delight in looking up the names of flowers, especially the wild ones. He was a changed boy since arriving at Stonebridge Manor and his greatest wish was to be adopted by Mrs M. Billy knew that was probably not going to happen but didn't say anything. His teachers were delighted with his progress too.

One day, when Jules and Eugene were out with their parents, Simon, Billy and Mickey walked back to the Moorheads' old house. It was securely locked, of course, but the shed wasn't, so they went inside and 'borrowed' some old folding chairs which they thought would be useful in the den. When not in use they would be kept in one of the outhouses at Simon's place.

They were sitting comfortably in the den when they heard a familiar voice on the towpath.

'It's Max,' shouted Billy, dashing out of the den without thinking. 'Max, hi, it's me . . . Billy.'

'Hello,' said Jim, who was pushing Max along the path, 'so you must be Mickey. Wow you've got a den down there.'

Simon emerged from inside the branches, which to be fair, gave little shelter having shed their leaves.

'It's supposed to be a secret, Billy.'

Max laughed, 'Don't worry guys, Dad won't tell, will you Dad?'

'Certainly not. I used to love a den when I was your age.'

'We've got Mickey with us, Max, you know, my little brother. He's a proper Club member now.'

Mickey frowned at the word 'little' as he was growing very fast and knew one day he'd overtake Billy in height.

'I suppose it's been difficult for Max to join in with you down there,' said Jim, 'but I have an idea. When will you be here next?'

'Tomorrow, probably, about ten.'

'OK, see you then.'

As soon as he was home, Simon checked with his Mum that he'd be free on Sunday morning, then called up Jules and Eugene on the new laptop he'd had for Christmas. He didn't say why, but asked them both to be at the den at ten.

On the dot of ten o'clock, the four boys and Billy were together and Billy had helped Simon bring the four chairs. Mickey sat on a log. Jim appeared, with Max, and Jules started trying to hide the den entrance.

'It's OK,' said Billy, 'He knows. He found us yesterday. He won't tell.'

Jim helped Max to stand, then picked him up, as if he was a lightweight, and carefully carried him down the steps to the riverbank.

'You hold on to him lads, and I'll go up and get his chair.'

Jim folded the wheelchair and took it down the steps and into the den. Then he helped Max take a few shaky steps and sat him down. The others were impressed with Max's progress and so pleased he was able to be with them.

'I'll come back at twelve and collect you Max. And if there's anyone around I won't give away your position.'

'Your Dad's great,' said Mickey once Jim was out of earshot. 'We never had anything like that.'

'Well now you have us,' Eugene assured him, 'and we won't let you down.'

Rewards and awards

By the Easter holidays, Max had managed to join the others several times and they even helped him to cast a fishing line. They told him about the big fish but didn't see it again. On one occasion Max actually caught a small fish, which made the others green with envy as they hadn't caught a thing. They managed to land it and Max felt its scaly skin and the size of it before they let it go back into the water.

Some days they would take Max to Mrs M's garden and let him feel the flowers and leaves. Mickey made him guess what they were by the touch. Once or twice Jim took the walking frame along and Max stood up and took a few steps along the path, which was now cleared of trip hazards. Mrs M brought them drinks and biscuits and invited Jim into her kitchen for a cuppa.

'Mrs M,' said Jim after he'd sampled her freshly baked fruit cake, 'I wonder if you might help me with something. I read in the local paper that the Council is giving out community awards to local people who have done good deeds. Max's friends have turned his life around and although he still has a long way to go, and might never get his sight back, he has had a far better life these past months than we could have hoped. If I nominate them for an award, would you second my proposal?'

'Of course, I'd be glad to. They've helped me a lot too, and just for a couple of pounds here and there. They are a real example to others. Just let me know how and I'll do it.'

It was in the second week back at school when Mr Duncan, the Headmaster made a special announcement at the end of assembly.

'Now I am very pleased and proud of what is about to happen.'

The curtains of the stage behind him opened and there stood the Mayor, Mickey with Mrs M and Max with his Dad. All of Mrs Twinstead's class looked at Billy, knowing Mickey was her brother.

'Madam Mayor, would you like to step forward and tell us what this is all about.'

'Good morning school.'

Some of the children replied with 'good morning Mayor', or for those who knew her, 'good morning Mrs Rogers'.

'Some of you may know that the Council is awarding honours to local people who have made a difference, who have gone out of their way to help others. I'm delighted to say that four members of this school, along with young Mickey here, from the primary section, have been given awards for the help they have given to Mrs May in her lovely new home and particularly to Max who doesn't attend this school but who has received a lot of help and friendship from the award winners. Come forward please, Julian Petts, Eugene Miller, Belinda Moorhead and Simon Derby.'

Billy grimaced at hearing herself called Belinda but followed the boys onto the stage. As they turned to face the assembled school, they noticed Sally, Dilys, Claire and Jennie at the back of the hall, clapping along with the pupils.

Jim stepped forward and told the school that following Max's accident and their move to the area, they were afraid Max would be lonely and a bit lost, but his new friends had included him as much as possible in their adventures.

He turned to the Mayor and thanked her and the rest of the Council for giving the award.

The Mayor handed each of them a certificate and a cheque for twenty pounds. They were also given a small medallion on a ribbon inscribed with the words 'Young citizen of the year'.

'Now school,' said the Head, 'please go to your lessons and I will take these wonderful students and our guests to the staffroom.'

Once in the staffroom the head asked the school secretary to bring coffee for the adults and squash for 'the youngsters'.

After a while the Head said, 'Well done you four but I mustn't keep you from your lessons. Billy, see that Mickey gets to his, too. Off you go, and I'm really proud to have you in my school.'

There was a hint of spring in the air at last, so that evening the entire River Club met at the bus shelter. Max said he'd been dying to tell them what his Dad had planned but was sworn to secrecy. They all agreed that being good and helping others gave them a real buzz and vowed to keep up the good work.

As they moved on across the bridge, Mickey suddenly shouted, 'Look at that big fish. Cor it's huge!'

'That's lucky,' chorused the others. The day had just got even better.